CAREER BOOK 3
15 Career-readiness Strategies
for Parents
of High School Students
With Special Needs

JIM HASSE

DEDICATION

To my mom, Eileen, one of my main mentors,
who, as an elementary school teacher in 1940
(three years before I was born), actively carried out her belief
that "nurture is more powerful than nature."

CONTENTS

ACKNOWLEDGMENTS

A special thank you to Peter Altschul, Fernando Botelho, Earl Brancel, Judy Ettinger, Floyd Harris, Pam Hasse, Nan Hawthorne, Mary Krohn, Nancy O'Connell, Liz Seger, Ruth-Ellen Simmonds, Don Storhoff, Mårten Tegnestam and Bob Williams – all of whom (among many others) have provided me with valuable guidance during critical moments in my career development.

WHAT I BELIEVE

Over the last 20 years, I have identified a range of time-tested strategies I believe parents can use to prepare youngsters with disabilities for the world of work.

I believe guiding parents in implementing these strategies on a wide scale will bring these two results:

- More people with disabilities will be ready for work.
- Employers will find more job candidates with disabilities who they consider qualified for open jobs.

That's why I seek non-profit and corporate partners which have wide, established connections with parents who are looking for the answers I can provide about how to help their youngsters with special needs prepare for meaningful careers.

My message: I believe people can put disability to work as a competitive edge in today's job market.

For a long time, those of us dealing with disability employment issues have realized that individuals with a disability can add a valuable perspective to corporate efforts in the mainstream business world.

That message has had a difficult time getting public attention, but that may be changing.

I believe we can now more confidently state this finding: Employees with disabilities are more likely to bring drive, focus and innovation to the workplace than their non-disabled counterparts.

Consider the following three contemporary authors who have recently brought those three "advantages" of disability employment to the public's attention through books which have received good reviews in the mainstream media.

First, in "The Triple Package: What Really Determines Success" (2014), Amy Chua and Jed Rubenfeld discuss the reasons behind personal achievement.

Successful people, they say, tend to feel simultaneously inadequate and superior. They:

1. Believe they are, in some ways, exceptional.
2. Are insecure about their worth or place in society – that they're not "good enough."
3. Resist the temptation to give up instead of persevering in the face of difficult circumstances.

They may appear to have a chip on their shoulders because they have a need to prove themselves.

For those of us with a disability, for instance, we may have a personal need to prove to others that we are the "exception" to commonly held beliefs within our society about people with disabilities in general.

I believe that inadequate/superior package tends to generate a personal drive in "overachieving" individuals with a disability – a need to prove oneself by sacrificing present gratification in pursuit of future attainment.

I must confess that this inadequate/superior duality fits me to a tee. For a thorough examination of that duality in me, go to the directory for my series of seven Amazon books about my personal transformation stories as a person with cerebral palsy at cerebral-palsy-career-builders.com/transformation-stories.html.

Second, Geoff Colvin sums up the power of deliberate practice with a purpose in his book, "Talent Is Overrated: What Really Separates World-Class Performers from Everybody Else" (2010). He writes:

> "...The most important effect of practice in great performers is that it takes them beyond -- or, more precisely, around – the limitations most of us think of as critical."

He pinpoints exactly why I believe it makes good business sense to hire people with disabilities who have developed the motivation to work hard at precisely the things they need to improve so they can contribute to a company's bottom line.

Colvin cites research that indicates what we think of as "innate talent" is more accurately termed "long-term, sustained practice at what really counts" driven by a passion to reach a goal (or in response to the triple package described above by Amy Chua and Jed Rubenfeld). In other words, Colvin says it's all about self-discipline no matter what the motivation.

Third, in "David and Goliath: Underdogs, Misfits and the Art of Battling Giants" (2013), Malcolm Gladwell offers a new interpretation of what it means to live well with a disability.

His main point: What is innovative, beautiful and important in the world often arises from what looks like suffering and adversity.

In other words, being an underdog can change people. "It can open doors and create opportunities and educate and enlighten and make possible what otherwise may seem unthinkable," Gladwell writes.

Gladwell even promotes the idea of a "desirable difficulty," such as dyslexia, a learning disability that causes much frustration for students as they learn how to read but, at the same time, forces them to compensate for that barrier by developing better listening and problem-solving skills – and by being innovative.

I encourage you, as a parent, to keep these considerations in mind as you help your youngster with special needs prepare for a meaningful job in an integrated work situation.

I researched and wrote the material for this book long before the afore-mentioned authors became popular. Over the last 20 years, I have gradually realized the importance of disability as the foundation for the resiliency of humankind throughout history.

However, only in the last five years have I publicly admitted that my disabilities, while they have made life tougher for me to live, have also, within certain contexts, become an aggregate advantage for me.

That reconciliation – and even love – of one's personal vulnerabilities perhaps come with age and the advantage of hindsight.

At any rate, please keep these initial remarks in mind as you review the following career-readiness strategies for your youngster. Your youngster's personal circumstances as well as the National Career Development Guidelines in the back of this book can also temper your thoughts.

Will your youngster be able to frame disability in such a way when he or she makes the transition from school to work that will help hiring managers recognize disability's competitive advantage?

Will those hiring managers seize the opportunity they have for boosting drive, focus and innovation in their workplaces by hiring your son or daughter?

I believe the answer to both of those questions can be "yes."

But, first things first. Your youngster needs to first grow in self-confidence.

STRATEGY 1 - DEVELOP EMOTIONAL INTELLIGENCE

I recently overheard this off-the-cuff statement:

> "…I started out mopping floors, waiting tables, and tending bar at my dad's tavern. I put myself through school working every rotten job there was and night shift I (could) find…"

Four questions popped into my head about that statement:

1. **What** makes a job "rotten?"
2. **Are** there any really "rotten" jobs out there?
3. **As a person** progresses through her career, when does she stop looking at every job she happens to have at the present moment as "rotten" because she's bored, feels unneeded and is attracted to the next level of responsibility -- perhaps at another company and in another industry?
4. **Is this person** displaying emotional intelligence?

My First Job

I believe we almost always learn something from each work experience – even in so-called "rotten" jobs, a term I didn't hear very often in the 1960s.

After graduating from college in 1965, for instance, I started working in a copy editing job. My "desk" was a foldable (and wobbly) card table in the back of the dingy break room where I had all-day access to the coffee pot and was frequently interrupted by co-workers who were ready for a 15-minute "party."

Many days I was discouraged because I felt caught in a "dead-end" job (and disliked coffee). But I also honed my writing and copy editing skills and learned newsletter layout during those first two years in the break room. It was not a "rotten" job. It was a job which provided the experience I needed.

Since I was gaining valuable experience on that entry-level job, why would I describe it as "rotten"?

Maybe it was because I knew it was another small step in my personal quest to build an independent life, admitting there would likely be many roadblocks to achieving that dream because of my CP. I knew, despite the disappointment and unpleasantness, that job would eventually be my passport to a meaningful career.

And it did. I ended up as vice president for corporate communication for that same company 20 years later.

I now feel lucky that I was able to recall the hours of rehab work I logged as a kid, learning how to walk in a straight line by putting one foot ahead of the other. I applied that routine (often exhausting but rewarding) to that first job and the other work situations which followed.

My Bias as a Hiring Manager

I also now wonder if I would hire anyone (disabled or not) who would voluntarily describe any one of their work experiences as "rotten." From my perspective, that's not "emotional intelligence." Would that person possess the insight, diligence and resiliency I need to strengthen my team? Or, would that person tend to be a job hopper and cost me time, money and effort by needlessly increasing my employee turnover?

I'd probably just go on to the next job applicant and look for someone who could concisely describe to me what he or she had learned from each work situation -- even mopping floors.

I'd be more impressed with someone who traces his current problem-solving ability in business to the experience of adapting to his disability -- such as substituting a mop for his crutches (and still maintaining his stability) while doing KP duty at his college fraternity.

A job applicant who describes one of his previous jobs, no matter how menial, as "rotten" or "crappy," would probably not make my top-three list of candidates for any open job because that individual has not shown me self-esteem or emotional intelligence.

I have three reasons for making that flat-out statement.

First, I ask myself, "Does this person recognize that people generally feel they have a right to equal dignity?"

Robert W. Fuller, former Oberlin College president and author of "Somebodies and Nobodies: Overcoming the Abuse of Rank" (new Society Publishers, 2003), defines dignity this way:

> "Dignity means equal recognition as human beings. People do not object to differences in rank -- only to abuses of those differences... They feel they have a right to equal dignity."

Fuller defines "somebody" with the perception of being "relatively powerful and successful."

But, "'Nobodies,'" he says, "are perceived as being relatively weak and vulnerable. Somebodies with higher rank and more power in any given context can maintain an environment that is hostile and demeaning to nobodies with lower rank and less power in that context."

He further explains, "Rankism occurs when rank holders use the power of their position for unwarranted benefits or advantages to themselves. It typically takes the form of self-aggrandizement and exploitation of subordinates. It is the opposite of service."

Fuller says, "...The familiar 'isms' (can) be seen as subspecies of rankism. Racism, sexism, Anti-Semitism, ageism and others all depend for their existence on differences of social rank that, in turn, reflect underlying power differences. So, they are forms of rankism."

Fuller also writes, "People do not really want or expect an egalitarian society because everyone recognizes how different we all are. But they feel they have a right to equal dignity. A central tenet of every religion, dignity would not be easy to campaign against."

My second concern: Does this job candidate have the essential self-esteem to function well on my work team?

If that person considers a previous time in his life as "rotten," he's essentially discounting his own experience. Such resentment for having to live through a work experience that may have been unpleasant indicates, in my mind, a diminished self-esteem.

Nathaniel Branden in his book, "Six Pillars of Self-esteem" (Bantam, 1995), says this:

> "To trust one's mind and to know one is worthy of happiness is the essence of self-esteem ... It is a motivator, more so than a feeling or a judgment; it inspires behavior ... How we act in the world and our level of self-esteem influence each other profoundly."

My third concern is this: Does this job applicant display the emotional intelligence I require of my team members?

According to Steven J. Stein and Howard E. Book in "The EQ Edge: Emotional Intelligence and Your Success" (Jossey-Bass, 2006), emotional intelligence is the ability of an individual to form optimal relationships with other people through a blend of hope, empathy, trust, integrity, honesty, creativity, resiliency, consequence-thinking, and optimism so he can build stronger social networks and manage difficult situations.

The main skill in emotional intelligence is delaying gratification in pursuit of long-range goals – and feeling good about it (instead of resentful).

When I was on the job on a hiring capacity, I looked for a sense of dignity, self-esteem and emotional intelligence in job candidates -- especially those who have honed such attributes by dealing effectively with a disability.

In doing so, I was giving myself the opportunity to choose self-confident people who, with emotional intelligence, could strengthen my team over the long haul.

Learning how to relate to others with emotional intelligent is an important self-confidence milestone for your high school student. It's definitely a career builder from my perspective.

STRATEGY 2 - COLLECT RESUME WRITING TIPS

Every few years, career counselors and hiring managers seem to come up with a new set of "preferred" resume writing tips. The latest twist is the recognition that generally people in this second decade of the 21st Century tend to develop "portfolio careers."

The "portfolio career" term recognizes that your youngster will not have one job or one employer during his or her lifetime but, instead, multiple jobs and multiple employers within one or more professions.

In fact, Robert C. Chope, Ph.D., says your soon-to-be job seeker can expect to spend about four years on one job and change jobs nine times during his or her career. That will put a premium on personal branding skills, which involves identifying a generic function your youngster performs within the work world. He or she then can become more specific about "what I can do" for particular jobs.

For instance, a "communicator" can be a "radio broadcaster," an "online blogger," an independent journalist," a "corporate communicator" etc., which all call for the same core skill set.

The "portfolio career" term also means your youngster will probably play many roles within one job (writer, teacher, manager etc.)

So, how will your youngster be able to explain -- in one resume -- all those roles to potential employers once he or she is in the job market?

Among contemporary resume writing tips is this tidbit: The answer may not be a chronological resume or a functional resume but a combination resume.

Here are the latest resume writing guidelines for a combination resume:

- **It combines** the chronological and functional formats by putting functions and skills at the top of the page and a reverse (earliest to latest employment record) chronological employment record at the bottom of the resume.
- **Unlike in the functional resume,** timelines are included, but marketable skills and accomplishments are highlighted and are upfront.

The biggest weakness of a combination resume is that it departs from the traditional format and is unfamiliar to many people. It's best used when there is a need to highlight flexible qualifications for a variety of jobs.

Other Resume Tips

Tony Beshara has been a top recruiter since 1973. He says today's hiring authorities typically want job seekers to clearly state, right up front, these bits of information in their resume:

- **Who** they have worked for (the company and the specific the division of the company).
- **What** that division does (products, functions, services etc.).
- **What** job they held (title and key responsibilities).
- **How** well they performed in that particular job for that division.

It's a tall order, particularly when you consider that 60 percent of the time resumes are not initially be read by someone with hiring authority but screened by an HR person or a machine.

But, I believe Beshara's advice has the elements of an effective resume guide for your future job seeker.

Resume Writing: Today's Realities

"Your resume is only a tool to get a job interview, which is the most important thing in getting hired," says Beshara, who has been featured on the Dr. Phil Show numerous times. "You are trying to get screened *in*, and HR is trying to screen you *out*."

During that initial process, your youngster's resume is likely to be scanned online (not read) for 10 seconds, he emphasizes. So, Beshara advises, your soon-to-be job seeker's work record needs to be in bold typeface, citing metrics to document results.

In other words, your youngster needs to learn how to document performance (even if it's for a volunteer position or part-time job) to do well in tomorrow's job market.

More than 80 percent of hiring authorities care less about a candidate's cover letter than the accompanying resume, Beshara maintains. They may read it after considering (and attracted) by the resume.

He points out that only about one percent of employers have a talent management system. Most use sites such CareerBuilder.com or Monster.com to post entry-level job announcements.

Here's the most important piece of advice for your youngster's future resume I believe Beshara offers:

> "Read the job announcement carefully, and identify the key words you find in that announcement which describe the qualifications for that job. Imbed those key words (and the concepts they imply) in your resume."

Beshara points out that today's employers usually make hiring decisions based on the relative weight of these four factors:

- **"We like you."** - 40 percent of the time.
- **"You're not a potential risk."** - 30 percent of the time.
- **"You can do the job."** - 20 percent of the time.
- **"We can work the money out."** - 10 percent of the time.

"You can't hope to establish a good rapport with a hiring manager through your resume," says Beshara. "That you can tackle during the interviewing process."

But, notice how high "risk" ranks in the decision-making hierocracy.

Risk assessment, says Beshara, is a key "screening-out" consideration that often happens at the resume-review stage of recruitment. That's a particularly important insight for your future job seeker with special needs.

"You need to recognize your barriers that may be evident through your resume as real risk factors," he emphasizes. "Have you worked too many years in one job or a one company? Does your resume portray you as 'job hopper?' Are there gaps in your employment history due to your disability? Have you been unemployed for a lengthy period of time?"

Those issues may not be of real concern now for your high school student, who may be just beginning to look for a part-time job, but, as the years go by and a job search becomes a crucial school-to-work matter, they can become important considerations.

It's often tough to address a personal barrier without first having direct, face-to-face contact with the hiring manager who is recruiting for an open job. A hiring manager can be more flexible than a screener in deciding why your youngster should be included as a candidate who gets a job interview, even though the apparent risk may be rather high.

Even without an apparent risk, Beshara adds, most job seekers today will probably not be called for an interview when they submit their resumes for a publicly posted job. In 35 to 40 percent of the cases, the decision makers involved have already decided to fill the job with someone inside the company or someone who is outside the company but in the hiring manager's network.

Resume Writing: What to Do (and Not Do)

Bottom line advice for your future job seeker who is compiling tips for writing a resume:

> Don't rely on your resume to get job. Avoid using it as a crutch by submitting it to job search sites and then think you're job hunting effectively. It's a poor way to look for a job. A job posted on CareerBuilder.com can easily get 500 resumes, for instance. Do you really want to compete with 500 applicants for a hiring manager's attention?

Blogging, making video resumes and gaining an online and social media presence can be helpful secondary tools in the job hunting process, but they can also be time wasters, blunting a job seeker's focus, according to Beshara.

Instead, Beshara recommends a more direct approach. Use an in-person network or LinkedIn connections to announce: "I'm interviewing at such-and-such company. Who do you know who can give me an inside picture of the company?"

Here are two other Beshara tips I find helpful and which you may want to add to your son or daughter's resume writing guide:

- **Study** the company's competitors. What does the company need to meet and beat its competitors? Customize your resume for that company, based on your research. Show how your track record has prepared you for meeting the needs of that hiring manager by relieving a pain or achieving a gain.
- **Take** the initiative. Once you've completed your research and polished your resume, telephone the hiring manager for the department and job you're targeting and say, "You need to hire me, and here's why. When can we meet?"

Beshara believes telephoning smaller employers (not just big companies) close to home makes sense. "There are 7.5 million companies in the U.S.," he says, "and 98 percent of them employ fewer than 100 people. In fact, the average U.S. company employs 16 people."

Yes, that's doable.

Helping your budding job seeker collect resume tips for future use, especially about how to avoid the "crowd," is a career and confidence builder.

STRATEGY 3 - BECOME FAMILIAR WITH TODAY'S WORK OPTIONS

"Where do I want to work?"

High school may seem a bit early for addressing that question, but it's not really premature, especially for your youngster with special needs. Your high school student needs to move beyond "fantasy careers" he or she may have envisioned at seven. At 17, the right career information just may be the jolt your youngster needs to start dealing with reality.

Your youngster can get the jump on other future job seekers by taking time to think about "Where do I want to work?"

There are basically seven answers to that question. When the time comes, your son or daughter can seek a job in a startup company; a small, well-established business; a large national and multi-national business; a non-profit/non-governmental organization; a local/state governmental agency; or in Federal government service. Or he or she can pursue self-employment.

There are advantages and disadvantages for each of these seven different types of workplaces -- ranging from job growth potential to everyday work flexibility.

Which workplace situation will be best for your youngster a decade from now? It depends on personal preferences when it comes to risk tolerance, on-the-job autonomy, career path development etc., but now's the time to start discussing the available career information which can make a difference between a frustrating first job out of school and one that is satisfying and motivating.

Let's take a closer look at the workplace choices available in terms of these five factors:

- Job growth
- Acceptance
- Accommodations
- Authority
- Compensation

Some of these factors have implications for your future job seeker as he or she deals with disability and the barriers it can put up in finding employment and doing well in a workplace.

Job Growth

In July, 2010, the Ewing Marion Kauffman Foundation released a study which shows net job growth occurs in the U.S. economy mainly through startup firms.

The study, "The Importance of Startups in Job Creation and Job Destruction," bases its findings on the Business Dynamics Statistics (BDS), a U.S. government dataset compiled by the U.S. Census Bureau.

The BDS series tracked the annual number of new businesses (startups and new locations) from 1977 to 2005. It defines "startups" as firms younger than one year old.

The BDS data shows that, both on average and for all but seven years between 1977 and 2005, existing firms are net job destroyers, losing one million jobs net (combined) per year. By contrast, in their first year of operation, new firms add an average of three million jobs.

Most notably, during recessionary years, job creation at startups remains stable, while net job losses at existing firms are highly sensitive to the business cycle.

On average, one-year-old firms create nearly one million jobs, while ten-year-old firms generate 300,000. The notion that firms bulk up as they age is, in the aggregate, not supported by data.

Citing the Kauffman study, John Tornius, chairman of Serigraph, a printing, molding, and custom graphics company in Milwaukee, WI, urges states and universities to "hug entrepreneurs" to help a region thrive by providing them with "angel capital" and start-up business expertise to keep them in the area. "They may eventually become a Microsoft, a Google or a Facebook, all startups started by college students," he notes.

"We're an innovation economy," he explains, pointing to the partnerships formed by universities and local entrepreneurs for the economic growth in such areas as Boston, New York City, Minneapolis, Austin, the Research Triangle, Seattle, Silicon Valley etc.

Tornius' bottom-line recommendation: Avoid "old industry" states. Search for startups in states which have highly paid young people; people in the "creative class;" high quality of life (recreation, arts etc.); and accessibility features that are essential for people with a variety of disabilities, he urges. Go to where the startup jobs are and where local, non-governmental groups are providing startups with support and money.

Those are bits of career information for high school students I wish I had in 1960 – or, better yet, my parents had because I was not yet thinking in those "global" terms when it came to making career decisions.

Acceptance

There's another reason your future job seeker may want to look for work in geographical areas which attract startup companies and the younger people who work for them. They may find more hiring managers who are not hampered by false assumptions about disability.

For instance, Generation Y (born between 1977 and 1995) hiring managers (both men and women) within small companies (particularly within the high-tech sectors) are generally more tolerant of diversity than previous generations in an American society where white males are no longer dominate the business landscape.

They are simply seeking individuals who can help them gain an edge over their competitors and colleagues, according to Jason Ryan Dorsey, author of "Y-size Your Business: How Gen Y Employees Can Save You Money and Grow Your Business."

Your youngster will need to capitalize on that opportunity for stepping beyond old stereotypes and bask in the acceptance he or she will likely find in tomorrow's workplace.

Accommodations

Small employers (particularly startups) often operate on extremely tight budgets and may not be held as accountable to ADA mandates as larger companies. So, here your youngster will have an opportunity to show his or her creativity, teamwork and problem-solving ability.

How about sharing the cost of any adaptive software your future job seeker might need with a prospective employer? Now's the time to research and keep abreast of new technologies which can make that possible. Make that a part of the career information for high school students (a good title for an e-mail file) you and your youngster collect.

At any rate, your youngster needs to be prepared to draw upon personal experience in offering potential solutions to any workplace accommodation he or she may need down the road during a school-to-work transition.

Authority

Unlike a federal or state job or a position in large company, a job in a startup may not be tightly defined. Your youngster could be more of a generalist, and individual authority may be unclear.

That means your son or daughter will need to thrive in a little bit of ambiguity, have a willingness to be flexible, be able to carry out a variety of functions (even though he or she has special needs) and live under a set of sometimes sizable but calculated risks.

In return, there's probably an opportunity for an industrious individual such as your youngster to create a slot for his or herself within a startup and take an important step in building a career.

But, the shining potential of a startup should never hide reality. Your youngster will need to carefully analyze each potential startup's capitalization, business plan, core offering, competitors, and corporate culture. Most importantly, he or she will need to assess the business acumen, the creativity, and the values of the principal players.

Notice the attributes your youngster needs in order to thrive in a startup: clear personal values, business acumen, good judgment etc. Now's the time to start developing those attributes.

Compensation

If your youngster eventually joins a startup company, he or she may receive a salary but more likely, at the beginning, be offered compensation of the more creative variety -- from stock options, deferred pay, stipends or even volunteer work (to show what he or she can contribute to the team effort).

You may want to remind your high school student that volunteering or working at a part-time job for a startup during college may be one way to "get a foot in the door" of a budding enterprise.

In short, startups need workers who are innovative and resilient and who can deal with ambiguity and risk -- attributes your youngster may be acquiring now while learning how to live well with a disability.

Such information can be crucial to your youngster's career development. If he or she is that type of person, a startup company may be the right step to take in making the school-to-work transition.

Just keep in mind this key point: Your youngster can get the jump on other future job seekers by taking time now to think about "Where do I want to work?"

STRATEGY 4 - REALIZE DISABILITY IS BECOMING IRRELEVANT

We're at the dawn of an age where people and machines are becoming one -- not just externally but internally (thanks to nanotechnology). With advances in medical technology, individuals previously thought to be "crippled," "handicapped" or "disabled" are becoming "perfectly able" and part of the employable population.

The Dawn of a New Age

Here are two visionaries who see the dawn of this new age: Raymond Kurzweil and Dr. Miguel Nicolelis.

Raymond Kurzweil, author, inventor and futurist, has been instrumental in helping people use technology to work around their disabilities. He has helped develop optical character recognition (OCR), text-to-speech synthesis, speech recognition technology, and electronic keyboard instruments.

He expects to see the combination and consolidation of three important technologies in the 21st century: genetics, nanotechnology, and robotics (including artificial intelligence).

In "The Singularity Is Near: When Humans Transcend Biology" (Viking, 2005), Kurzweil asserts that medical advancements will make it possible for a significant number of his generation (baby boomers) to live long enough for the exponential growth of technology to intersect and surpass the processing of the human brain.

Just think what that means for your high school youngster.

If transcending our biological limitations becomes reality, then everyone will be unable (a disability) to compete effectively without the intervention (an accommodation) of technology. Today's most common definition of "disability" (a condition which limits one or more of a person's life activities) will be meaningless and obsolete.

Dr. Miguel Nicolelis is a Brazilian physician and scientist best known for his pioneering work "reading monkey thought" and using brain-computer interface (BCI). In 2008, Nicolelis's lab saw a monkey implanted with a new BCI successfully control a robot walking on a treadmill in Kyoto, Japan. And, that propelled him into a project he calls as significant as putting a man on the moon.

By capturing brain function, Nicolelis is paving the way for a cure for Parkinson's disease, new ways of treating paralysis, and using brain waves to control "whole body" robots for helping people with no mobility to walk.

Named by "Scientific American" as one of the 20 most influential scientists in the world, he is the professor of Neurobiology Biomedical Engineering and Psychological and Brain Sciences and co-director of the Center for Neuroengineering at Duke University.

See Nicolelis's new book, "Beyond Boundaries: The New Neuroscience of Connecting Brains with Machines -- and How It Will Change our Lives" (Times Books, 2011).

New Definitions

The work of both men prompts me to ask:

- **Will** your high school student be in the unique position to show that disability is, indeed, disappearing as a concept once he or she becomes a part of the employable population 10 years from now?

- **Will** aging become a process in which we accumulate accommodations to continue to refine, use and share our seasoned skills with others well past the traditional "retirement age?"

We could be on the cutting edge of a new way of looking at aging, disability, and special needs -- and what constitutes the employable population.

And, we could be reaching a point in the near future where virtually everyone will need an accommodation (such as a computer today) to effectively compete in the workplace, enjoy recreation to the fullest and obtain a meaningful education.

If that's the case, disability is disappearing for those of us living in the 21st Century. Disability doesn't matter anymore in terms of accessing the means to fully participate in society.

Death is also taking on a new meaning. Death is being "disabled," the point at which combining a human being with machines to be "perfectly able" is no longer feasible or preferred.

What You Can Do

That's the exciting future your youngster with special needs faces today. Explore, with your high school student, the new advances in technology as they come on stream. Together, become "armchair experts" of what is happening in neuroscience, genetics, nanotechnology, robotics and artificial intelligence. It's fun. It builds self-confidence.

As "disability is disappearing" evangelists, you two can demonstrate the inadequacy of our current definitions of disability and what we currently consider the employable population.

And, as an "accommodation guru," your high school student can grow into a valuable resource person who can help prospective employers continually tap the technology those with disabilities and those without need in order to work effectively and efficiently in the 21st Century workplace.

Also remember that tomorrow's smart employers will be actively recruiting those who are personally harnessing technology to make disability irrelevant. Those job seekers who are part of today's "disability is disappearing" revolution will likely be the innovators tomorrow's businesses will desperately need to compete effectively in the global marketplace.

STRATEGY 5 – EXPLORE POST-SECONDARY OPTIONS

In 1961, I didn't have many post-secondary options. Tech schools were still geared toward the industrial age. Universities and colleges emphasized liberal arts and required a "classroom presence."

It was also before the Americans with Disabilities Act (ADA) and Section 504 of the Rehabilitation Act (section 504).

As a new high school grad, I had earned a four-year state scholarship from Wisconsin pre-DVR services, and I was excited about getting my degree in journalism from the University of Wisconsin-Madison.

I remember going to the Madison registrar office on Bascom Hill ready to apply for school, only to find the admissions people wouldn't accept me because they believed I couldn't climb the hills and steps on campus to make it between classes.

Reluctantly, I agreed to take my first two years of classes at the then Wisconsin State College at Platteville, a smaller, flat campus. I earned straight "A's" and then was finally accepted as junior at Madison, where I could obtain my journalism degree.

During the summer after my sophomore year, I learned how to use Canadian crutches in the fields of our home farm, timing my pace each day so by that fall I knew I could even climb the Bascom Hill steps to get to class in times within the 15-minute break between sessions.

Looking back, I could have used today's options in education as well as the curb cuts and elevators now mandated by the ADA. I could have also used an electric scooter, my Amigo, which, at the time, was not yet on the market.

Today's Situation

Today's colleges and universities are struggling to discover how to define themselves in an educational environment where virtual learning is becoming increasingly commonplace and lectures by the most distinguished professors are available online.

I'm curious to see how brick-and-mortar campuses are going to adjust to this new reality of students worldwide having a virtual learning option.

Check AccreditedOnlineColleges.org, a general information website with many resources useful to all people looking to further their education. This site discusses the offline and online educational paths your youngster can follow to obtain a degree from an accredited institution.

Another helpful site is OnlineSchool.org, which allows users, for free, to search and locate all non-profit higher education institutions with online course offerings.

I also recommend this article: "Accredited Online Colleges and Disability Education," which is a quick summary of the situation as it exists today for individuals with disabilities.

Pros and Cons from my Perspective

Here's how I view the advantages and disadvantages of virtual learning.

Advantages of Earning Online Degrees:

- Expenses for a dorm or an apartment are eliminated.
- There are fewer hassles and easier access for those with mobility and other accommodation issues.
- There's an increased opportunity to access the best programs and lecturers.
- Scheduling classes and learning time is more flexible.

- Individualized attention by instructors is more convenient and time efficient.

Disadvantages of Earning Online Degrees:

1. Online degrees may have less prestige within the work world.
2. Students may miss the experience of living independently for the first time.
3. Students may miss day-to-day, face-to-face interaction with people from different cultures and backgrounds.
4. Students may miss the synergy of in–person group activity which often generates innovative entrepreneurial opportunities.
5. Students may miss important in-person learning experiences which provide individual feedback and build teamwork skills.

Deciding whether to join the trend toward online degrees depends on the personal preferences, educational goals and career objectives of your son or daughter. That's why it's important to discuss these issues now, while he or she is still in high school.

Having an expanding variety of options available for post-secondary education, however, should be confidence builder for you, as a mentor, and your youngster.

STRATEGY 6 - KNOW HOW TO SET GOALS

Goals need to have substance. They must be connected to your youngster's values.

Imagine for a moment that your youngster has the desire to be a computer network administrator for a medium-sized company. How can he or she embark on this journey (which will likely entail years of training and hands-on experience) without making plans? Without establishing goals, how would your youngster know when he or she had achieved that dream?

Your high school student needs to practice these two steps for effective goal setting: "Where am I going?" and "How do I get there?"

Effective Goal Setting Asks, "Where Am I Going?"

In the business world, job seekers succeed because they know where they want to go. It is essential to set both short-term and long-term goals in a sequence that shows where they're going. These goals become more potent and more easily attainable when they are aligned with personal values and driven by a personal vision.

So, effective goal setting for your high school student starts with exploring and understanding personal values, the guiding principles for your youngster's personal and eventual working life.

When I was 14, I knew I wanted to write as a vocation because, for me, writing was a way to increase understanding (my personal value) within a diverse group of people. That understanding would help people work together more effectively (my vision).

Your youngster's values and vision are closely tied to his or her personal interests, one of the drivers of career development. Observation and casual conversation over the years can give you a good idea of what your youngster values most when it comes to a vocation: challenge, security, relaxation, renewal, adventure, an exotic environment etc.

Examples of values include excellence, honesty, innovation, spirituality, respect, and authenticity. Help your youngster think of values as guiding principles: what he or she wants and needs in a personal and work life.

Help your youngster make a list of values. Then, together, look for patterns and ways to group individual values together.

After reviewing my list of values as a 51 year old, for instance, with the help of a career coach, I grouped them into three distinct categories – learning, adventure, and communication. My communication category included creativity, authenticity, and connecting.

The next step is to create a clarifying statement, blending the values that your high school student has grouped into a category. Let's continue to use my communication example. I developed the following clarifying statement:

> "I value effective communication. It's an essential part of who I am, both personally and professionally. Authenticity is an important part of communication for me. I strive to be authentic in the way I connect with others. I value life-long learning, and I continually work to sharpen my writing and strategic communication skills."

Your youngster's clarifying value statements can play a key role in the development of his or her personal brand.

For instance, I brand myself as a "disability employment expert who helps individuals put disability to work as a competitive edge in today's job market." That's my 15-second elevator pitch, a reply I can use when I'm asked, "What do you do?"

My statement often leads to this question: "How do you do that?"

My standard response:

> "I walk the people I coach through a series of career builders so they can gain the confidence they need to deal effectively with disability employment issues."

But, in today's world, even my 1980s elevator pitch is too long. So, now I use three words to describe what I do: "Showing Disability Works."

Effective Goal setting Asks, "How Do I Get There?"

Goal setting is the methodology by which individuals can systematically support their success. Accomplishing goals helps to create and sustain that success.

As your youngster begins to develop goals, guide him or her through the following questions:

- Is there something that needs to be completed?
- Do you have a concern that is unresolved?
- Do you have an unfulfilled dream?
- What things should have had a higher priority this last year?

When establishing a goal, our popular culture likes to cite the SMART principle:

- **Specific:** Be very specific in writing a goal.
- **Measurable:** Develop criteria to measure progress and success.
- **Attainable:** Be sure the goal is realistic and attainable.
- **Relevant:** Consider personal values. Is it relevant?
- **Time Bound:** Establish timeframes.

But, Dr. Samantha Collins, CEO of Aspire Companies and founder of The Aspire Foundation (a mentorship program for women across 24 countries), is not a big fan of SMART goals, especially for high school students.

She recommends, instead, "developing more of a vision, going to your highest level."

She adds, "You don't have to be realistic at this stage. Your vision should invoke excitement as well as slight terror -- terror because you're clueless about how you're going to pull it all off. All the planning can come later."

In my case, I always had my values in my heart and my vision in my head. But, I could never make SMART work as an effective goal setting process because it didn't seem to be helpful for me.

Instead, embracing happenstance, being open to change and knowing my end point (being able to live independently) seemed to work well for me. In short, I'll admit that I "winged it" until I reached middle age.

I have a hunch that whichever effective goal setting track your youngster finds helpful will depend on his or her temperament. But, just being aware that effective goal setting is part of developing a meaningful career – and that there are choices in how to do that -- is a confidence builder.

STRATEGY 7 - LEARN HOW TO DIFFUSE STRESS

Does your high school student know the ground rules for bringing less stress to a situation?

An affirmative answer to that question could eventually prove to be your son or daughter's competitive edge when he or she makes the transition from school to work.

"Knowing how to manage your personal stress level and clearing the way for others around you to be less stressed are marks of a leader and a measure of social intelligence," according to Jordan Friedman, MPH, The Stress Coach, a nationally recognized stress management and health promotion speaker and consultant.

Both attributes (leadership and social intelligence) are key attributes employers seek in job candidates.

Friedman has his own stress-to-success story.

In the fifth grade, he was diagnosed with one of the largest brain tumors ever discovered. After brain surgeries, years of extreme vision loss, and pretending to be "normal," he went on to become a public health expert who now uses his experiences to motivate others to deal productively with life's challenges, changes and crises.

He's an expert at avoiding anxiety, calming down quickly, seeking quality support and sleeping more soundly.

Friedman says leadership within a work environment is essentially being aware of the "pinch points" which cause stress and knowing how to reduce such tension through effective observation, listening, communication and problem solving.

Disability as a Double-edged Sword

Over the years, I've found my CP is a double-edged sword when it comes to workplace stress. It can either hurt or help a situation, depending on how well I handle the anxiety others normally feel when they meet me for the first time.

How I project myself -- and ultimately appear to others -- can be a barrier or a unique stress-reduction personal brand. If I appear to others as a stress reducer, then it's another personal attribute I can use to show why I'm the better candidate for a particular job.

I'm a stress generator (increasing the stress level of an entire team) if I'm a complainer, if I choose not to interact effectively with my colleagues by keeping to myself, if I shirk off my job responsibilities to others, if I get visibly upset each time another person reveals a false perception about CP or if I try to take advantage of my disability in gaining special workplace privileges. I'm stressed, and my stress affects the entire team.

Contrast those stressors with one simple stress reducer we can all employ: listening to others.

"I think people with disabilities have more experience in solving problems and dealing with crises than the average non-disabled person," writes Peter Altschul, a Missouri-based consultant on the psychology of change and former diversity manager at Reuters News Service who happens to be blind.

"I have discovered that people will say things to me that they wouldn't say to other (managers)," Altschul relates. "Maybe it's something to do with their perception of our 'semi-invisibility' -- that those of us with disabilities are sometimes ignored as if we aren't present -- and, therefore, are 'safe' listeners to unguarded remarks."

It's like having a built-in GPS at the upper ranks of an organization for locating what employees, at all levels and on an anonymous basis, are really feeling. Retrieving, accepting and acting on feedback are marks of senior management's effectiveness in leadership.

I have also leveraged that phenomenon periodically in my own corporate communication career to benefit upper management. Otherwise guarded people at every level within an organization sometimes felt free to speak candidly with me, even though they knew I was a part of senior management.

Stress-reducer Ground Rules

Flip 10 years into the future. Imagine the impact a discussion about your youngster's skill as a stress reducer could have on a hiring manager's decision once he or she has reached the second or third interview of the hiring process.

The ability to reduce stress within a work team could be the clincher. It could put your young job seeker into the position of being hired.

Your high school student needs to start preparing now for what will be required when he or she starts hunting for a job. That means, upon accepting a job, he or she must be prepared to:

- **Be** candid about disability. Ask the supervisor for an appropriate time to discuss it at a staff meeting.
- **Gain** an understanding with the supervisor that, "I was hired because of my qualifications to do the work at hand, and I expect to satisfy the same performance standards of my colleagues." It means working with the supervisor to reinforce that understanding in the minds of co-workers.
- **Assure** the supervisor that, "I will not play a passive or manipulative role on the work team. Appropriate discussions concentrate on what I can do and how -- not what I can't do." That means making sure responsibilities within the team are well defined and equal.
- **Show** the supervisor that, "I want to be treated like everyone else on your team (which means neither ignoring nor highlighting me because I happen to have a disability)."
- **Realize** that employees will often have false perceptions about disability (maybe based on previous experiences with individuals who did not know how to handle their disability appropriately in a workplace situation). That means helping the supervisor be prepared to deal with those false assumptions, which often are simply due to lack of information. Request that, as a new employee with a disability, "I'm not to be judged until I have had time to establish myself as a member of the team."

- **Work** with the supervisor to encourage a relaxed atmosphere that includes humor but does not tolerate stereotyping, bigotry, or mean humor.
- **Make** sure a person taking on new duties is adequately compensated in some way for them if the supervisor must shift a responsibility from one job description to another because of your youngster's special needs. Higher pay or authority (or simply allowing for an exchange of tasks) can make the addition acceptable so it doesn't breed ill will between your son or daughter and that person.
- **Work** with the supervisor to make a list of ideas about how to reduce your youngster's stress (and that of the supervisor and co-workers) during the first three months of your youngster's new job.
- **Make** sure venues for routine social interaction with co-workers are accessible, especially if they are off-site. Your son or daughter will need to make it a point to participate in those social interactions.

Friedman maintains there is no upside to ignoring stressors and no downside to preventing or resolving them. In fact, neglecting to give stress its due attention will most certainly result in a greater negative impact than that of any time taken to prevent that tension.

So, now's the time (while in high school) for your youngster with special needs to learn how leveraging a disability can diffuse stress. By doing so, your high school student will eventually be more prepared to get hired precisely because he or she has proven to be a leader with social intelligence.

STRATEGY 8 - DEVELOP PROBLEM-SOLVING SKILLS

Informed recruiters within many of our nation's leading companies know the following statement to be true.

Employees with disabilities who are effectively recruited, trained and promoted bring to workplace teams these qualities:

- **Reduced** missed days of work.
- **Lower** turnover.
- **Increased** awareness of and appreciation for unique customer needs.
- **Proven** problem-solving skills.

Together, these attributes add up to increased productivity, the real bottom-line benefit of including individuals with disabilities in our nation's workforce. It means that employers with the savvy to find talented job seekers with disabilities who can show work results based on these high-in-demand but often low-in-supply personal qualities will likely be the most successful in the years to come.

But, let's not stop there.

The New Reality

Your high school student with a disability needs to recognize that today's employers are facing at least three new recruiting problems, according to John Liptak, Ed.D., Associate Director Career Services, Radford University, Radford, VA.

Here's how Liptak describes these recruiting challenges:

- **Employers** are unable to fill vacant jobs.
- **Employers** are not able to hire workers with the required skills.
- **Jobs** are changing so quickly that workers need basic skills for a variety of tasks.

Why are jobs going unfilled when our nation's unemployment is so high?

Liptak has been studying the survival and success rate of people entering the workforce since 2006. He says the U.S. workplace is still in a transition from what he calls the "traditional" model to a "high performance" model. The "employability" skills required for this new work environment have changed as a result, but our educational system is not fully preparing future job seekers for those changes.

In May of 1990, a U.S. Department of Labor committee launched a comprehensive study about how well schools prepare young people for the workforce. Titled the Secretary's Commission on Achieving Necessary Skills (SCANS), this extensive work gave American businesses, for the first time, a platform to clearly communicate to educators what students need to know in order to be successful in the workplace.

The SCANS Report concluded that "... more than *50 percent* of our young people leave school without the knowledge or foundation required to find and hold a good job."

Obviously, that caused quite a stir in education because school boards, administrators, and teachers realized our nation's students were not learning what they needed to know in order to be prepared for the workforce of the 21st century.

This problem, the report said, stems from the fact that today's working environment, focused on information, service, and communication, is vastly different than the industrial workplace of the early 1900s – due, in part, to advances in technology and competition from countries abroad.

The report called for a whole new approach to education, involving a switch from basic-skill learning to development of thinking skills and problem solving skills.

Yesterday's traditional workplaces were centrally controlled and marked by mass production and fragmented tasks performed by employees who had minimal qualifications and training and who were encouraged to "specialize" in their careers. Advancement was by seniority.

Today's high-performance work environment is characterized by flexible production, decentralized control, work teams, and multi-skilled workers. Training is available to anyone, and advancement is based on certification of skill sets.

In short, today's employers are seeking employees with thinking skills and individuals who work well with others (and learn with others) so they can use their problem solving skills to effectively address a series of issues on a variety of projects.

And, increasingly, individuals find themselves "hiring out" their problem solving skills on a contractual basis to a variety of "employers."

Liptak observes that there are still "deficits" in thinking skills, resource management, information skills, interpersonal skills and systems management – all what the SANS Report calls "employability skills" (skills which are not technical but which cut horizontally across all industries and vertically across all jobs).

One example of an employability skill is the ability to work cooperatively with others to solve real issues.

The SANS Report has prompted 45 states to adopt Common Core State Standards, the educational approach that is overhauling classroom instruction. Common Core State Standards emphasize critical thinking and problem solving and are meant to better prepare students for success.

Filling the Void

Anytime I see a gap between need and capability in the general labor force, I see opportunities for future job seekers such as your youngster who are fully prepared to fill that void.

For employers, I also see an opportunity to fill that void by recruiting talented, prepared individuals with disabilities, a largely untapped resource with only *37 percent* of working-age adults with disabilities participating in the labor force (according to the U.S. Bureau of Labor Statistics.

And, for some occupations, this gap is being filled by savvy, talented individuals with disabilities. For example, the employment rate for scientists and engineers with disabilities is *83 percent*, much better than the estimated *37 percent* for the overall U.S. population with disabilities, according to the American Association for the Advancement of Science.

In fact, pursuing a STEM career (such as process engineer, which uses knowledge of science, technology, electronics and math in integrated ways) is well worth the effort. It fits the new paradigm of multi-skilled employees who work under decentralized authority and who can transfer their problem solving skills among a variety of occupations and industries.

Process engineering jobs, by the way, often go unfilled due to lack of qualified applicants.

If there are jobs open because there are not enough people qualified with the new "employability skills" to fill them, those are the jobs for which I would prepare and seek – particularly because, as a person with special needs, I have learned how to effectively manage my disability by working with others. And I know how to transfer those attributes to on-the-job situations.

Look at a few of the key skill deficits Liptak says he still finds in individuals entering the workforce. I'll give you examples of how your youngster with special needs can eventually cite work/volunteer/care management experience for turning those nation-wide deficits into personal competitive advantages he or she can use to get hired.

- **Thinking Skills** – "I creatively came up with technology-based solutions to address my walking and talking disabilities by visualizing preferred outcomes, learning about the options I had and carrying out the steps needed to realize those outcomes."
- **Personal Qualities** – "I have effectively managed a series of paid personal assistants during the last five years with integrity and authenticity through honest, open communication."

- **Resource Management** – "I managed time, money and materials in a six-month advocacy effort for people with disabilities who were in need of local transportation services."
- **Technology Use** – "I chaired a committee which studied and recommended note-taking options to add as a disabled student service at a local, private college."

Notice these so-called new employability skills are competencies that stem from the four productivity attributes I first listed above. These competencies have already been proven, though decades of study, to be qualities an employer gains by hiring individuals with disabilities.

So, what was true in the last century is even more so in the 21st. A strong workforce includes individuals who have acquired problem-solving skills by learning how to live well with disability.

Employers will likely find that kind of flexibility and ingenuity in tomorrow's job candidates with special needs, who have learned, through success and failure, how to live with ambiguity on a daily basis. Learning how to live with personal ambiguity makes working under a rigid job description unnecessary.

Your youngster with special needs experiences first-hand a range of disability-related variables, some threatening and some just simply annoying but all often requiring a snap decision. He or she probably is in the habit of using creativity (and personal judgment) to deal effectively with vulnerability and ambiguity.

In tomorrow's business climate, people who do not need to be wedded to restrictive job descriptions are the type of workers who will be in demand. They will continue to provide the extra spark for an organization's innovation.

It's a personal marketing approach your youngster can eventually use in seeking a job. In using that approach, he or she will be acknowledging the gap between the need and availability of key employability skills (such as problem-solving skills) and adding those competencies to his or her portfolio.

I see no better strategy than positioning oneself as a job candidate with proven problem-solving skills. It's putting the right frame on disability's competitive edge.

STRATEGY 9 - PLAY THE "EXCEPTION" TRUMP CARD

It's time to acknowledge that, although many employers are fully committed to hiring, retaining and advancing qualified individuals with disabilities, the perceptions of some employers about a variety of important disability employment issues haven't changed much since the passage of the Americans with Disabilities Act (ADA) of 1990.

The Good News

Don't be discouraged, though. Your high school student is in a unique position to change perception one person at a time. You can help him or her prepare for the role of an educator during job searches.

The task is to show prospective hiring managers he or she does not fit their preconceived notions of a person with a disability -- that your mentee is indeed the "exception" to sometimes long-held beliefs.

That means your youngster must begin to actively position him or herself as the exception to those misconceptions, which are usually based on lack of knowledge. Those false impressions may have roots in misunderstandings picked up during the hiring manager's childhood. They have never been challenged in the hiring manager's mind -- until the individual you're mentoring appears as a job candidate.

Here's the good news. Getting hired is not crucial at this point. As a career coach, you have time to counsel your high school student, and he or she has time to learn these basic problem-solving strategies for addressing misconceptions about disability.

Since misconceptions usually stem from lack of information, you have an opportunity to counsel your high school student in showing he or she doesn't fit the hiring manager's preconceived notions. That tends to "unfreeze" job interview situations so your "now-grown-up kid" can go on to explain why he or she is the best candidate for the job at hand.

Those problem-solving strategies of selling yourself as a job candidate who is the "exception" and the best candidates in terms of qualifications came back to me as I recently reviewed an important study of the attitudes, beliefs and practices of U.S. employers.

U.S. Dept. of Labor's Employer Attitudes Survey

According to the National Council on Disability's "Achieving Independence: The Challenge of the Century," the most commonly cited reason for not hiring people with disabilities is a "lack of qualified applicants." That's closely tied to another reason I commonly hear: "the inability to locate or find qualified job applicants with disabilities."

Google "Attitudes of Employers: Findings From the Most Extensive Survey in History of Employers' Actions and Attitudes Toward Employing People With Disabilities."

Here are some clues from that survey that you may find helpful in career coaching your high school student with special needs about problem solving-strategies.

- **Larger** companies are more likely to actively recruit people with disabilities (33.8 percent) than smaller companies (7.8 percent).
- **In absolute numbers,** there are more mid-sized companies (164,460) recruiting people with disabilities than small (96,052) and large companies (66,209).
- **The nature** of the work being such that it cannot be effectively performed by a person with a disability is cited as a hiring challenge by 72.6 percent of all companies. Attitudes of co-workers or supervisors are the least frequently cited challenges.

- **Health care costs**, workers compensation costs and fear of litigation are more challenging for small and medium companies than for large companies.
- **The cost** of employing people with disabilities and the belief that workers with disabilities lack the skills and experience necessary are the most often cited concerns for small and mid-sized companies, while supervisor uncertainty about how to take disciplinary action is cited most often for large companies.
- **The services** of Job Accommodation Network (JAN) are familiar to only 7.4 percent of companies. Large companies are much more likely to be familiar with JAN services than are small and medium-sized companies (21.6 percent compared to 6 percent and 5.9 percent, respectively). Public administration employers are more likely to be familiar with JAN (19.2 percent) than are employers in service (7.3 percent) or goods-producing industries (6.2 percent).
- **Information** about satisfactory job performance, increases to the company's productivity, and benefits to the company's bottom line were the three most persuasive reasons for hiring people with disabilities. But small and medium companies find information about satisfactory job performance most persuasive, while large companies are most persuaded by information supported by statistics or research.
- **Large companies** ranked inability to find qualified people with disabilities as their number one challenge.
- **Not knowing** how much accommodations will cost and the actual cost of accommodating disability are major concerns associated with hiring people with disabilities.
- **Public administration** organizations tend to actively recruit and hire people with disabilities more than their private sector counterparts.

I believe these results show why you need to help your high school student with special needs take the time now to practice the lone "educator" role as part of the future task of finding full-time employment.

The mission for your son or daughter: Educate one potential employer at a time (instead of trying the change the whole world's perception of job candidates with a disability) by proving, "I'm the exception to the common rule you've been taught." That's your youngster's disability edge.

STRATEGY 10 - IDENTIFY A TEAM ROLE THAT HAS THE RIGHT FIT

Youngsters with special needs will be steps ahead of their able-bodied competitors in finding a part-time job now and an entry-level job after school, if they can find, at an early age, what role they can best play in a team effort.

That's why volunteering for a service organization or just working as a member of the homecoming committee as well as holding several paid, part-time jobs while in high school are so important. Each work experience gives youngsters an opportunity to discover their "teamwork voice."

In fact, taking risks, building self-esteem, flexing leadership muscles, developing business savvy and building solid at-work relationships are all essential building blocks for developing an effective teamwork presence for the workplace.

Which Profile Fits your Youngster?

But, there's also another, faster way for youngster to develop a teamwork voice -- even at the high school level.

Allen Fahden and Srinvasan Namakkal studied teamwork for decades. Their Innovate with C.A.R.E. Profile (now called Team Dimensions Profile®) can help your youngster identify his or her potential role in a team setting.

According to Allen Fahden and Srinvasan Namakkal, successful team members do the right thing at the right time -- not the same thing at the same time. While team members work together toward a common goal, individuals still must play their individual parts in the process.

Fahden and Namakkal's instrument helps individuals identify their most natural team role so they can work from their strengths. The Team Dimensions Profile®, a product of Inscape Publishing Inc., a leading provider of DiSC® assessments, is available through authorized distributors of Inscape's products, including Teambuilding, Inc. and The Center for Internal Change.

Here's a glimpse at the components of Fahden and Namakkal's original Innovate with C.A.R.E. Profile:

Creator
- Generates fresh ideas and original concepts that often defy generally accepted rules.
- Is not constrained by fear of failure.
- Hands off tasks to an Advancer.

Advancer
- Recognizes new ideas in the early stages.
- Chooses the direct and most efficient means to achieve objectives.
- Hands off tasks to a Refiner.

Refiner
- Challenges concepts and ideas, often playing the "devil's advocate," to detect flaws and potential problems.
- May hand ideas and plans back to an Advancer or a Creator before handing off tasks to Executor.

Executor
- Lays the groundwork for implementation in an orderly, well thought-out manner.
- Prefers that others take the lead but enjoys the responsibility of final implementation.

Facilitator
- Monitors how well individual team members are contributing to the team effort.
- Identifies the need for hand-offs from one role to another.

You often hear a Creator say, "I have an idea," while an Advancer might say, "I hear an idea I like." The Refiner will likely tell you, "I can poke holes in your idea so you can make it better," while the Executor often volunteers to gather the information so the idea can be implemented. The Facilitator on your team is your "deal maker," who is concerned about handing off the team spotlight from one role to another at the right time.

A balanced team (one where the members complement one another) is more likely to achieve breakthrough performance, according to the creators of the Team Dimensions Profile.

Watch your high school youngster interact with friends, play games, participate in sports and solve problems with the help of others. It'll give you a hint of how he or she will eventually react to situations where teamwork in the workplace is essential.

Here's is one situation that could tell you a lot about where your youngster fits in the Team Dimensions Profile. Does your youngster actively participate within an informal, temporary team of vendors, counselors and funders while choosing the right adaptive equipment needed to do well in high school? If so, is there a noticeable difference in how your youngster functions in one of these roles: creator, advancer, refiner, executor or facilitator? Is she or he more noticeably comfortable in one of those situations?

When the opportunity presents itself, help your youngster recognize various team roles and which are a "natural" for him or her. Doing that during high school will prepare your youngster for the transition from school to work.

Remember, prospective employers (even at the burger-flipping level) are seeking to balance their teams. Youngsters who recognize that need for teamwork in the workplace and have the savvy to show how they can fit in will have a "leg up" on other job candidates.

At that point, your youngster's ethnicity, gender, sexual preference -- and special needs -- will be irrelevant.

STRATEGY 11 - FOLLOW A PLAN FOR MAINTAINING MOTIVATION

The days and weeks may slip by with no tangible success as your high school student tries to land that "dream job" for the summer or for the semester.

Such a situation can be particularly daunting when disability is involved as an extra barrier to employment. As a person with CP, I know that "sinking feeling" when nothing seems to provide the edge you need to break into "mainstream" employment, even at a part-time level.

The good news is that, after looking back on 45 years of employment, I recall mostly the bright spots in my career -- when things did seem to work well for me in the long run. The "dark days" and all the extraordinary effort it often takes to start (and build) a meaningful career as a person with CP seem to fade in my memory.

How can you help your youngster to keep trying (and always be positive) when he or she is getting no response or outright rejection by employers?

I now believe that your youngster's dark days don't have to be so dark, if you help him or her to remain open to adopting a motivation plan. That means pursuing some of these seven ways to battle discouragement while landing that important first-time job during high school:

- Form a mentorship.
- Form a mastermind group.

- Volunteer with a purpose.
- Become job market savvy.
- Think of the job hunt as an adventure.
- Document success.
- Feed a network.

I'll explain what I mean by each of these elements of a motivation plan for your youngster.

Form a Mentorship

Become a mentor (instead of a "mom" or "dad" or "uncle" or "aunt" or "grandma") for your youngster. Meet in person on a routine basis. If meeting in person is not possible, rely on Skype e-mail and text chat for one-on-one communication.

As a mentor, you should be able to level with your youngster on an adult level and honestly tell him or her when things look like they're going well -- and when they're not -- in coping with the part-time job search. You are the key to making this motivation plan succeed.

Form a Mastermind Group

Encourage your youngster to form a mastermind group with at least two other fellow job seekers, perhaps students from the same high school. A mastermind group is simply an alliance of two or more individuals dedicating themselves to a specific goal – in this case getting temporary work.

The key to creating a successful mastermind group is for group members to agree on a set of rules or guidelines that assure the continued success of the group.

Two rules stand out above all others. They are: Show up for your meetings or calls and participate with an attitude of, "How can I be of service to the other members of my group?"

When your youngster commits to supporting a mastermind group, the very best thing he or she can do is show up for the call or meeting. One person's absence from the group will significantly change the dynamics of the group.

Your youngster's attitude should never be, "Here's what I need." A mastermind group is based on unconditional service to others within the group. By supporting others in the group, your youngster will receive support.

This does not mean your youngster goes to a mastermind meeting with the thinking, "There's nothing I need help with. I'm only here to help you." Being vulnerable and open to suggestions is part of the mastermind process.

Volunteer with a Purpose

Encourage your youngster to volunteer doing work he or she intends to pursue as a career. If she's into accounting, urge her to volunteer to help a non-profit with its accounting work. If he wants to be a teacher, encourage him to volunteer as an aide in one of your local schools.

Your youngster needs to select volunteer work carefully, choosing situations in which he or she has a clear job objective, clear guidelines and a clear understanding of expected results and how work will be evaluated in terms of performance.

Within those parameters, your youngster will more easily be able to cite his or her volunteer work experience as a significant qualification for a specific part-time job during interviews.

Gaining needed work experience through volunteering can be an important driver within any motivation plan.

Become Job Market Savvy

Encourage your youngster to become knowledgeable about his or her particular field as well as the labor market in general. Talk about what your youngster is finding.

About 30 years ago (before the Internet), I became very familiar with the jobs available in my field, the qualifications employers were seeking and the salaries being offering by studying the want ads in major newspapers and professional periodicals and networking (in person) with people in my field at national conferences and local association meetings.

That was part of my motivation plan.

Think of the Job Hunt as an Adventure

Your youngster can approach this first job hunt as a research project for exploring what works and what does not work in terms of results. That means charting findings and progress and sharing those with family and friends, who can become the "cheer and support" group within your youngster's motivation plan.

To do that, your youngster needs to set up a system (perhaps using a simple spreadsheet) for recording the date, time and nature of each initiative he or she takes as part of the job search, noting results.

Over time, your youngster can focus efforts on the marketing channels (which social media, for instance) are giving the best results. That means he or she is continually refining the job marketing campaign.

Show your youngster that sharing results with significant others in a network will keep those network members engaged in his or her job marketing campaign.

It worked for me. I landed my first job through an off-the-cuff recommendation from my uncle.

Document Success

Encourage your youngster to keep a diary about what he or she is learning about the job hunting process and about his or her personal growth as a job seeker. Reviewing those accounts of success regularly will set a job marketing pattern early on, and that will be helpful later in making the transition from school to work.

Sharing success stories now with family and friends and periodically tweaking them will eventually help your youngster become comfortable recounting them in job interviewers when appropriate.

Feed a Network

People close to your youngster want to see him or her succeed, and they'll help, if they know what they can do to help. So, keep extended family members involved and give them up-to-date information about how the job hunt is going through e-mail, social media etc.

Most of all, give them the tools they need to highlight your youngster's availability in their conversations with others. That means always giving them easy access to your youngster's resume, online portfolio and wish-list of employer contacts.

Bottom line: Your youngster doesn't have to be alone in his or her job search. In fact, trying to do it alone can be disastrous. Instead, help your youngster use his or her personality and insight to engage others in helping find that first part-time job.

These seven ways to battle discouragement can help your youngster effectively cope with tough situations due to disability while in high school. But, they can also become a template for addressing challenges throughout his or her career whenever "the chips are down" – a leverage that can provide a competitive edge in an eventual transition from school to work.

STRATEGY 12 - USE CAREER CLUSTERS TO GUIDE CAREER PLANNING

Career clusters are a useful guide in developing programs of study in high school and beyond so your high school student can plan fields of study for a complete range of career options.

As an organizing tool for curriculum design and instruction, career clusters provide the essential knowledge and skills for 16 career pathways.

The 16 career clusters in the National Career Clusters™ Framework, representing more than 79 career pathways, can help your high school student with special needs navigate his or her way to success in college and in career building.

Those guidelines were first introduced by The National Association of State Directors of Career Technical Education Consortium, which was established in 1920 to represent the state and territory heads of secondary, postsecondary and adult career technical education across the U.S.

Let's look at one career cluster. Here's the career cluster definition for Science, Technology, Engineering and Mathematics (STEM) careers:

> "Planning, managing, and providing scientific research and professional and technical services (e.g., physical science, social science, engineering) including laboratory and testing services, and research and development services."

That career cluster definition may not mean much to you, me or the high school student you're mentoring, so I'm going to cite a concrete example (a profile) of a STEM job.

Let me introduce you to Jack, a real person I know who works as a process control engineer in the paper industry. I'm masking his true identity so I can give you more inside information about Jack, his job and his company that would otherwise be difficult to disclose.

Job Types

In practice, process control engineering takes one or more of the following forms:

> **Discrete** – Robotic assembly, such as in the automotive industry, is an example of discrete process control. Most discrete manufacturing involves pieces of product, such as metal stamping.
>
> **Batch** – One example is the production of adhesives and glues, which normally require mixing raw materials in a heated vessel for a period of time to form an end product, such as a food, beverage and medicine.
>
> **Continuous** – The control of the water temperature in a heating jacket is an example of continuous process control. Some important continuous processes are the production of fuels, chemicals, paper and plastics, usually in large quantities.

As control engineer of a continuous process, Jack monitors all processes in a large pulp paper mill, which, since 1996, has continually developed its capability, in incremental steps, to control its paper-making process through computer technology.

Job Demand

Jack is one of two process control engineers employed by the mill, which converts pulp wood into a range of high-grade papers. The pulp mill's manager said the company would like to hire another process control engineer, but it has not been able to find such a qualified individual. Most large paper mills throughout the world employ two to four process control engineers.

Many U.S. colleges place process control engineer specialists immediately upon graduation due to a high demand in the manufacturing industry, according to degrees.info.

Skills Needed

Since there are so many departments involved in process controls, clear and concise communications are imperative for a process control engineer to be successful. Jack has had to develop his team leadership skills and be able to independently make decisions.

Project management is a large part of his job. Upon completion of each of his projects, detailed documentation from inception through completion is required.

Jack is often required to perform a myriad of tasks in a typical workday.

As project goals and guidelines are altered by supervisors on the production floor and by technical roadblocks, he must be able to accurately assess the situation. He then must present alternate solutions based on his knowledge and experience as well as that of his colleagues.

Education Needed

As one of the 16 career clusters, STEM careers, such as process control engineering, apply science, technology, electronics and math (STEM) in a systemic approach to a workplace challenge.

In Jack's case, he attended a well-regarded four-year campus of a major state university and earned a double major in computer science and electronics and a double minor in physics and math. He had three computer programming internships at a single, local company during his four years of college.

Upon graduation from college, Jack expected to get a job consisting mostly of programming because career clusters and STEM careers had not yet moved to the forefront of America's educational system. But, by happenstance, he discovered the process control field used all of his STEM disciplines of science, technology, electronics and math.

Job Tasks

Jack uses computer technology to monitor the entire process throughout the mill as well as all the associated utilities. He's also charged with the responsibility to fine-tune the controls for the entire paper-making process or at specific sections of the system.

That means he needs to have knowledge of electrical systems and instrumentation. He must know how to write code as well as understand valve, flow meter and boiler technology (specialty knowledge he has picked up through continuing education since he started working as a process control engineer in 2006).

Jack's "office" has a high-tech ambiance. He works with three large monitors and a variety of processors which allow him to control or watch all the vital control systems throughout the mill.

With an access of up to six different electronic "highways" within the mill, he can call an on-the-floor operator to tell him or her that a valve with a specific unit, for instance, is not operating properly.

He always has the option to walk the floor himself, which he often does, to speak with operators in person, but that is not necessary.

Compensation

According to glassdor.com, the average salary for a process engineer in the paper industry is $98,000.

Skill Transferability

Jack is interested in physical therapy and fitness. He has recently realized that he could apply these same skills and knowledge to physical therapy or in various sectors of the health care field in addition to any process that transfers a raw commodity (such as iron ore into steel, milk into cheese, cotton into cloth, silicone into plastic, grapes into wine) into a finished value-added product.

Pay Back

Jack's mill manager considers the job of process control engineer as a "line" function (as opposed to "support" work), one that is directly related -- and can be easily traced -- to the company's bottom line results.

For example, Jack says his most rewarding work is helping a supervisor to examine the process variations within a particular work unit's output and to fine tune the computer code involved for optimum operating results.

In one particular instance, he recently helped the mill save $500,000 a year in operating costs by working with a supervisor to achieve a more optimum flow rate.

Accessibility

Jack's mill manager says the duties of a process control engineer could very clearly be carried out by a qualified person with a physical disability, since the work is done at a keyboard and going onto the processing floor during trouble-shooting episodes is "optional" in most cases.

High school is the time to help your son or daughter with special needs to explore all 16 career clusters and the more than 79 career pathways that are attached to them. Notice the required knowledge and skills and the potential pathways for each and any potential accessibility issues.

Knowledge about career clusters can give your youngster a competitive advantage when the time comes to look for that first "real" job.

STRATEGY 13 – UNDERSTAND INGRAINED FALSE ASSUMPTIONS

I believe your youngster with special needs will need to go into the mainstream job market with an understanding of what he or she faces in terms of the following six barriers -- false assumptions which can, at times, be formidable barriers to landing a meaningful job.

- Bias
- Presumption
- Myth
- Skepticism
- Prejudice
- Discrimination

All but two of these barriers (prejudice and discrimination) to your youngster's eventual employment can be knocked down through education and information sharing.

That's why your youngster needs to prepare now for these two important roles: effective job seeker and savvy educator. Your high school student will not only need to find the job with the right "fit" but also recognize and work around those six potential barriers by showing hiring managers that "I'm an exception to your assumption of what job applicants with disabilities can and cannot do on the job."

Here's how I approach each of these "enemies." Consider my approach and then select the tips you may want to pass along to your high school student when the right opportunity presents itself.

That process may eventually help you both develop your own discrimination definition (the "biggie," which can be a guide in deciding if personal rights have been violated).

Bias

Bias causes a person, most often unknowingly, to *influence a decision unfairly through partiality or favoritism.* An example would be a job application form a small business has created with no alternative formats that effectively acts as a barrier for a job applicant who has a visual impairment or who has difficulty with handwriting.

Bias is most often due to lack of information or insight. It can be corrected through information, education and training.

I would recommend, for instance, helping that small business discover the variety of options available today for allowing people to apply for a job -- from a website form or a CD of the form to an e-mail application etc. In doing so, I'm assuming the role of mentor and educator.

Presumption

Prejudice (see below) most always says something is *going to happen.* Presumption, on the other hand, says a thing *will probably happen.*

A hiring manager may assume, for instance, that your youngster with special needs would not be interested in a job which requires considerable travel time. It will be up to your future job seeker to anticipate such a presumption, if traveling extensively is not a problem for him or her.

Myth

Florida State University's Student Disability Resource Center identifies three common myths that most of us with a disability have encountered at one time or another. They are:

- **The Myth of the Helpless Invalid** (which assumes that the person with a disability is unable to do anything without assistance).

- **The Myth of the Heroic Cripple** (which places the person with a disability on a pedestal, making it difficult for him or her to assimilate and function).
- **The "Spread" Phenomenon** (which generalizes from a single disability and assumes there are also intellectual, social and additional physical deficits). An example would be shouting at a person with a visual impairment.

I've found the best way to deal with each of these myths is to immerse myself in a mainstream workplace and "educate" my colleagues -- one by one -- about who I really am

Skepticism

Skepticism is *uncertainty*. A hiring manager may not be certain that your youngster will be able to carry out a job's responsibilities.

The task your youngster needs to eventually carry out: Show hiring managers that, "Yes, I'm quite capable of doing the job."

More than likely, that hiring manager is thinking, "If I were in your shoes with your type of disability, I'd find it very difficult to do this job." It'll be up to your son or daughter to address this skepticism upfront. My recommendation: Prove, by citing experience, that "I'm perfectly able to do the job."

Prejudice

Prejudice infers *something is wrong* or that *something will surely happen*. It's as an opinion formed without the facts and is often an unreasonable position of a hostile nature. Prejudice is an unwillingness to change a personal attitude in the face of *overwhelming evidence* that a certain belief is false.

A prejudiced person may often present biased and inaccurate statistics to support an unfavorable opinion, generalization or feeling he or she has formed beforehand without knowledge, thought, or reason.

An example of prejudice is a person who refuses to hire people with disabilities because they "always require accommodations that cost too much, and the ADA law always backs them up no matter what kind of accommodations they say they need."

But, that's not yet a discrimination definition.

If, during the next decade, your youngster actually encounters a hiring manager who is, indeed prejudiced, I'd recommend refusing to spend time, money and effort in trying to deal with him or her.

There are plenty of other employers who are truly disability friendly and know that it makes good business sense to hire people with disabilities.

Discrimination

A discrimination definition under federal and state law is an act or failure to act in favor or against a person based on personal prejudice. It can be intentional or unintentional. A discrimination definition involves taking away an individual's personal rights.

Prejudice, on the other hand, is the *thought* of trying to be mean, devious, or evil.

In other words, if an individual actually *does* or *does not* do something based on personal prejudice, that act falls under the discrimination definition. If a person only *thinks* about doing something about a perceived problem but does not act on that thought, that's prejudice.

In either case, I would not spend valuable job-seeking time with people who are discriminatory or prejudiced or display bigotry, which is the stubborn and complete intolerance of any creed, belief, or opinion that differs from one's own. There are plenty of disability friendly companies which have good track records of hiring and promoting talented people with disabilities.

Human beings are understandably uncomfortable with disability because, most likely, they have not yet had first-hand experience with such vulnerabilities. And, many of us rely on long-outdated misconceptions we all pick up, at some point, during childhood.

Overcoming those ingrained false assumptions (particularly, by definition, discrimination) may seem like an almost impossible task.

But, it's important that your youngster begins to understand that he or she does not have to change the world singlehandedly. To eventually get hired, your high school student will only need to help one hiring manager in one company look beyond disability and recognize, instead, your youngster's attributes and potential.

Discovering Disability's Competitive Advantage

STRATEGY 14 - KNOW ADA'S BASIC PROVISIONS

High school is the time for your youngster with special needs to start understanding the basic provisions of the Americans with Disabilities Act (ADA) of 1990 and which job interview questions can and cannot be asked under the provisions of that law.

Here's a quick set of unfair, questionable and fair job interview questions, based on Equal Employment Opportunity Commission (EEOC) guidelines, which enforces provisions of the ADA.

Help your youngster understand these indicators now so he or she will be able to quickly determine whether an interview experience is on the up-and-up or dipping below the fairness (and illegal) level under the ADA

Unacceptable Application or Interview Questions

- "Do you have a physical or mental disability which would interfere with your ability to perform this job?"
- "Have you been hospitalized recently?"
- "How many days were you sick last year?"
- "Have you ever filed for worker's compensation?"
- "Have you ever been injured on the job?"
- "What prescription medications do you currently take?"

Under Title I of the ADA, your future job seeker can't be asked about the existence, nature, or severity of a disability. It prohibits questions about medical conditions; past hospitalizations; nature and severity of a disability; and other related matters on job applications and in job interviews.

By the way, the ADA does not require employers to give your son or daughter a hiring preference just because he or she has a disability.

But, the law prohibits an employer from refusing to hire or promote or from taking other adverse action against a person because of the person's disability, *if he or she can perform the essential functions of the job.* The law applies to private employers with 15 or more employees and to state and local government employers.

However, an employer can, under the law, choose a person without a disability with more experience over an individual with a disability, even if the individual with the disability is qualified for the job.

An employer can choose a person without a disability over an individual with a disability, if the two individuals are equally qualified, as long as the choice is not made because of the individual's disability.

The ADA prohibits employers from asking questions that are likely to reveal the existence of a disability before making a job offer (the pre-offer period). This prohibition covers written questionnaires and inquiries made during interviews as well as medical examinations. However, such questions and medical examinations are permitted after extending a job offer but before the individual begins work (the post-offer period).

Employers may ask an applicant these questions after making a job offer as long as they ask the same questions of other applicants offered the same type of job. In other words, an employer cannot ask such questions only of those who have obvious disabilities. Similarly, an employer may require a medical examination after making a job offer as long as it requires the same medical examination of other applicants offered the same type of job.

An employer may tell all applicants what the hiring process involves (for example, an interview, timed written test, or job demonstration), and then ask whether they will need a reasonable accommodation for this process.

If the employer believes an applicant with an obvious disability will need a reasonable accommodation to do the job, it may ask the applicant to describe or demonstrate how she would perform the job with or without reasonable accommodation.

A Fair Question

Here's a fair question employers can ask during a job interview under provisions of the Americans with Disabilities Act:

- "Can you perform the basic functions of this position with or without accommodation?"

Employers may ask your future job seeker whether he or she can perform the job-related functions as long as they don't phrase the questions in terms of disability.

For example, if driving a vehicle is a function of the job, the employer may ask if your youngster has a driver's license. However, the employer may not ask if having a disability prevents your son or daughter from driving.

A "Questionable" Question

- "Why is there a gap in your employment history between 2005 and 2007?"

Under the ADA, potential employers cannot ask certain questions at a job interview that would result in the applicant revealing information about the existence or nature of a disability.

Questions about gaps in employment history are likely to lead to information about an applicant's disability and are, therefore, arguably illegal. However, until the courts and EEOC clarify the issue, the law on this question is unsettled at the time of this writing.

How to React to Unacceptable Questions

Unfortunately, some employers persist in asking questions that are prohibited under the ADA. This places job applicants in the uncomfortable position of deciding how to respond.

My advice that you can pass along to your youngster is this: If you choose not to discuss your disability during the job interview, try to determine what type of information an employer is seeking through her line of questioning.

For example, an interviewer may ask: "What is your usual schedule on a typical work day?" You may deduce that she wants to know if your son or daughter would be missing work due to personal care issues, transportation problems etc. Here's a simple reply: "I'll have no problem meeting the position's attendance requirements."

If your youngster's main goal is to pursue the job, then I'd recommend refusing to answer a question in a non-confrontational manner. For instance, "I've read about a law that prohibits questions of this type during job interviews." This allows your future job seeker to avoid answering the question without giving the employer the impression that he or she has a disability, if your youngster chooses not to disclose because disability isn't obvious.

If your youngster's main goal is to get the employer to change an illegal interview process under the ADA, then filing a complaint with the EEOC or state or local human rights agency is in order. Ask the agency to take up the problem of the illegal question with the employer.

In short, prepare your youngster to judiciously use the leverage provided by the ADA when the time comes to seek employment.

STRATEGY 15 - DEVELOP A STRATEGY FOR DISCLOSING DISABILITY

When to disclose disability (on a job application, on a resume, before a job interview etc.) can come up as soon as your youngster fills out his or her first job application for that part-time work.

This disability disclosure issue goes far beyond the job application. And there are no easy answers, especially if your youngster's disability is largely "hidden." Yet, every job seeker with a disability eventually needs to personally come up with a strategy for addressing this matter.

As a career development facilitator, I tell my clients this: "When to tell prospective employers about your disability depends on your disability, your job opportunity, your personality and your prospective employer."

Remember, under the Americans with Disabilities Act (ADA), your youngster is *not* required to disclose his or her disability to an employer, even though it may just be a mom or pop candy store down the street.

And, if and when your youngster does disclose, he or she is not required to tell *everything* about the personal aspects of a disability. In other words, once your youngster discloses a disability. a potential employer can only ask for limited information about that disability.

In any case, when your youngster does disclose his or her disability, he or she needs to be prepared to provide just the basic information about limitations and about accommodations needed. That applies to simply completing a job application as well as performing essential job functions and receiving equal benefits and privileges as an employee.

Upon request, information about disability can be confidential. Your youngster's co-workers do not need to know about his or her special needs.

With those guidelines in mind, consider these three potential disclosure strategies, which are largely mutually exclusive. Each option largely stands on its own, has important advantages as well as disadvantages and should be applied only after careful examination of your particular situation and of the potential employment situation.

At any rate, the options may give you some ideas about how to coach your youngster in deciding when and how to disclose disability under a variety of employment circumstances.

Strategy 1: Getting your Foot in the Door First

Don't reveal your disability on your job application, resume or cover letter (even if you have gaps in your work experience due to your disability) because it will potentially trigger preconceived, inaccurate notions about disability among the people screening resumes for the open position.

Eliminate achievements or associations on your job application and resume which may reveal your disability.

Instead, do everything you can to get your foot in the door for job interviews, and, if your disability is visible, try to put your interviewers at ease early on in the process, assuring them that you have the skills to do the job.

Benefit:

You're more likely to have an even chance of getting through the initial screening process.

Drawback:

You're surprising your potential employer or job interviewers, who, at first, may be so preoccupied by your disability, if it is visible, that you'll have a difficult time helping them focus on your qualifications for the job. And the employer will not be prepared to provide you with any accommodations you may require at the time of your interview.

Needed Preparation:

Let your confidence and out-going personality shine. Show you can control an awkward situation. Be prepared to handle a variety of reactions. Weave your disability into the entire interview, showing how it has prepared you for meeting the work requirements and helping the company extend its success.

Strategy 2: Disclosing as Soon as Possible

Include a "Personal Statement," a few paragraphs in length on a separate sheet or document, with your resume. In this statement, briefly describe your disability and explain what adaptive strategies you use to get your work done.

Benefit:

Briefly describing your disability upfront may help your interviewers become comfortable with you more quickly, giving you more time to emphasize your skills and attributes (what you can offer instead of what you perhaps need in terms of accommodation).

You're informing your potential employer about your disability right off the bat, and, in doing so, you're putting the focus on how you're able to do the job. The employer can be prepared for the accommodation you may require at the time of your interview.

Drawback:

For employers who are not truly inclusive and not truly disability friendly, you may be setting yourself up as a job candidate who, in effect, is saying, "Don't bother considering me for this job. You have plenty of other qualified job candidates without a disability."

Needed Preparation:

Carefully craft you "Personal Statement" so it not only describes your disability and accommodation needs but also shows why disability has helped you acquire the qualities you have discovered, through company research, that are high on the list of your targeted employer's needs.

Strategy 3: Framing Disability as an Advantage

Instead of selecting an option for when to reveal your disability to a prospective employer (as though your disability always has to be a negative factor), turn the table 180 degrees. Position your disability experience as your competitive edge and target employers who claim to be disability friendly.

Consider what you've learned by adapting to (and living well with) your disability as part of your functional experience and link those lessons to the development of your accomplishments and skills.

That will give you ideas about how to develop your personal narrative as a job seeker around your disability experience. Use your personal narrative to drive your entire job marketing campaign (your resume, your offering statement, your portfolio, your company research, your networking and your job interview preparation). It can even drive how you complete a job application.

Benefit:

You're taking the initiative to show so-called disability friendly employers how your disability-honed experience has strengthened your problem-solving ability, your resiliency and your emotional intelligence -- attributes that are valued by employers and that give you an advantage over other applicants for a specific job.

By doing so, you may discover a golden opportunity in an organization which realizes that hiring people with disabilities is good business.

Drawback:

You're taking a calculated risk and will probably be rejected or ignored by employers who are not truly inclusive and not truly disability friendly.

Needed Preparation:

Incisive company research is important here. You need to network to find which companies on "disability friendly" lists are really all-inclusive or just there to make a good showing and meet

U.S. Equal Employment Opportunity Commission (EEOC) requirements.

You need to know yourself and why your disability experience is relevant to today's workplace. And, you need to know how to explain the connection between disability experience and workplace success in simple and concrete terms that are meaningful to hiring managers.

Those are the options I believe your high school student with special needs faces as he or she struggles with this sometimes-tough disability disclosure issue that crops up as soon as his or her first job application needs to be completed. Which to choose boils down to personal preference and personal situation.

But, choosing a course of action with personal capabilities, job, employer and competitors in mind -- and following through with that strategy -- is essential to getting hired in today's part-time job market (and tomorrow's mainstream workplace).

SUMMARY

Preparing for a meaningful career as a high school student with special needs can seem overwhelming at times. But, as a career-coaching parent, you can help your youngster do just that by focusing on these key strategies:

Growing in Self-confidence

Strategy 1: Develop Emotional Intelligence - Learning how to relate to others with emotional intelligent is an important self-confidence milestone for your high school student.

Strategy 2: Collect Resume Writing Tips - Helping your budding job seeker collect resume tips for future use, especially about how to avoid the "crowd," is a confidence builder.

Strategy 3: Become Familiar with Work Options - Your youngster can get the jump on other future job seekers by taking time now to think about "Where do I want to work?"

Strategy 4: Realize Disability Is Becoming Irrelevant - Job seekers who are part of today's "disability is disappearing" revolution will likely be the innovators tomorrow's businesses will desperately need to compete effectively in the global marketplace.

Strategy 5: Explore Post-secondary Options - Having an

expanding variety of options available for post-secondary education should be confidence builder for you, as a mentor, and your youngster.

Strategy 6: Know How to Set Goals - Whichever effective goal setting track your youngster finds helpful will depend on his or her temperament. But, just being aware that effective goal setting is part of developing a meaningful career – and that there are choices in how to do that -- is a confidence builder

Discovering Disability's Competitive Advantage

Strategy 7: Learn How to Diffuse Stress - Knowing the ground rules for bringing less stress to a situation could eventually prove to be your youngster's competitive edge when he or she makes the transition from school to work.

Strategy 8: Develop Problem-solving Skills - Picture your youngster as a future job candidate with proven problem-solving skills. That's putting the right frame on disability's competitive edge.

Strategy 9: Play the "Exception" Trump Card - The mission for your son or daughter: Educate one potential employer at a time (instead of trying the change the whole world's perception of job candidates with a disability) by proving, "I'm the exception to the common rule you've been taught." That's your youngster's disability edge.

Strategy 10: Identify a Team Role with the Right Fit - Prospective employers (even at the burger-flipping level) are seeking to balance their teams. Youngsters who recognize that need for teamwork in the workplace and have the savvy to show how they can fit in will have a "leg up" on other job candidates.

Strategy 11: Follow a Plan to Maintain Motivation - These seven ways to battle discouragement can help your youngster effectively cope with tough situations due to disability while in high school. But, they can also become a template for addressing challenges throughout his or her career whenever "the chips are down" – a leverage that can provide a competitive edge in an eventual transition from school to work.

Strategy 12: Use Career Clusters for Guidance - Knowledge about career clusters can give your youngster a competitive advantage when the time comes to look for that first "real" job.

Strategy 13: Anticipate Ingrained False Assumptions – Your mission is to help your youngster understand that he or she does not have to change the world singlehandedly. To eventually get hired, your high school student will only need to help one hiring manager in one company look beyond disability and recognize, instead, your son or daughter's attributes, capabilities and potential.

Strategy 14: Know ADA's Basic Provisions - High school is the time for your youngster to start understanding the basic provisions of the ADA and which job interview questions can and cannot be asked under the provisions of that law.

Strategy 15: Have a Strategy for Disclosing Disability – Deciding which disability disclosure option to follow -- and following through with that strategy -- is essential to getting hired in today's part-time job market (and tomorrow's mainstream workplace).

I wish you much success in carrying out these 15 key career-building strategies for your high school youngster.

NATIONAL CAREER DEVELOPMENT GUIDELINES

According to the National Career Development Guidelines (NCDG), these are the competencies your youngster can develop at the "knowledge acquisition" level during high school:

Understand that discovering one's personal interests, likes, and dislikes is a step toward building and maintaining a positive **self-concept**.

Show respect for **diversity** as an essential positive interpersonal skill.

Recognize that growth and **change** are essential parts of career development.

Achieve a **balance** among personal, leisure, community, learner, family and work roles.

Recognize that **educational** achievement and performance levels are needed to reach personal and career goals.

Realize that ongoing, **lifetime learning** enhances one's ability to function well in a diverse and changing economy.

Discover that creating and managing a **career plan** is essential to meeting career goals.

Start making **decisions** within an overall personal strategy for managing a career.

Recognize the importance of accurate, current and unbiased **career information** in planning and managing one's career.

Accumulate fundamental knowledge about the variety of **skills** that are important for success and advancement in school and work, such as communicating, critical thinking, and problem solving.

Realize that changing employment **trends**, societal needs and economic conditions have an impact on one's career path.

ABOUT JIM HASSE, THE AUTHOR

Jim Hasse is the founder of <u>cerebral-palsy-career-builders.com</u>, the comprehensive career coaching guide for parents of CP youngsters 7 to 27 years old.

He owns Hasse Communication Counseling, LLC, which helps champions of disability employment form partnerships for win-win direct mail fundraisers.

As a Global Career Developmental Facilitator (GCDF) since 2005, he's the author of 12 Amazon eBooks, each of which explains his central premise: that disability, when framed correctly, can be a competitive advantage in today's job market for job seekers with special needs.

To access his books in electronic as well as soft-cover formats, see http://tinyurl.com/JRH-All-Books-Amazon.

Hasse developed an award-winning corporate communication function for Foremost Farms USA, Baraboo, WI, during his service of 29 years at the cooperative -- 10 of which were at the vice presidential level.

Between 1999 and 2009, he was responsible for all the online content of eSight Careers Network, New York City. As eSight's senior content developer, he wrote, assigned and edited more than 1,300 articles about disability employment issues.

Between 1997 and 2001 (before blogging became commonplace), Hasse developed, facilitated and marketed tell-us-your-story.com, a now discontinued web site where people with disabilities shared their personal-experience stories and which provided a launching pad for eSight Careers Network.

A 1965 honors graduate of the University of Wisconsin-Madison's School of Journalism, Hasse is an Accredited Business Communicator (ABC) by the International Association of Business Communicators, San Francisco, Calif.

In 1994, he received the Cooperative Spirit Award from the Cooperative Communicators Association (CCA), a national organization for professional communications employed by cooperatives, and the Cooperative Builder Award from a state-wide association of cooperatives in Wisconsin.

In 1995, he received CCA's H.E. Klinefelter Award for distinguished service in cooperative communications.

In addition to his eBooks and soft-cover books, Hasse is the author of "Break Out: Finding Freedom When You Don't Quite Fit The Mold" (Quixote Press, 1996). a memoir of 51 short stories about disability awareness.

He also compiled and edited "Perfectly Able: How to Attract and Hire Talented People with Disabilities" (AMACOM, 2011), a disability recruitment guidebook for hiring managers that highlights disability's competitive advantage in today's job market.

JIM BOOKS

7 TRANSFORMATION STORIES

**Quick Career-insight Series of Seven Little Books
for Parents of Youngsters with CP**

Each of the seven Little Books takes about 40 minutes to read. Each illustrates and summarizes the essential career builders for your youngster's age group – all through seven transformational stories about Jim Hasse's personal experience as a person with CP.

You'll find considerably more detail about each career builder at cerebral-palsy-career-builders.com, which can be used as an ongoing reference for "how to" information as your youngster matures.

Buy **Little Book 1** on Amazon
at- http://www.amazon.com/dp/B00DPLHRTI

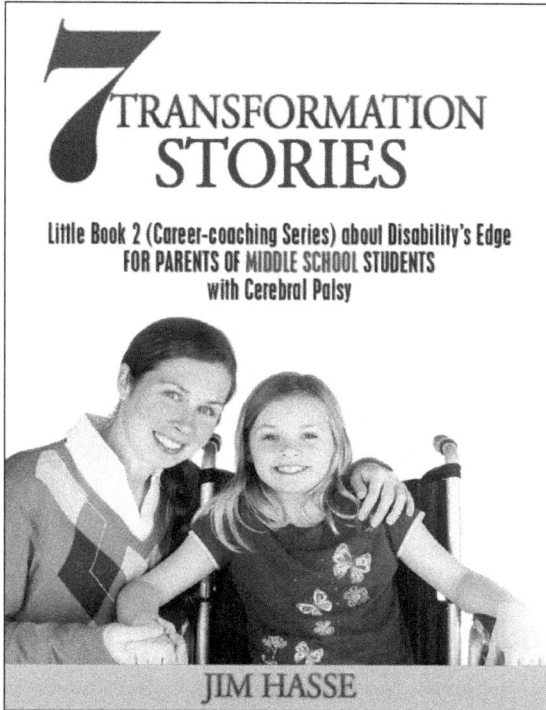

Buy **Little Book 2** on Amazon
at http://www.amazon.com/dp/B00H9WAKHA

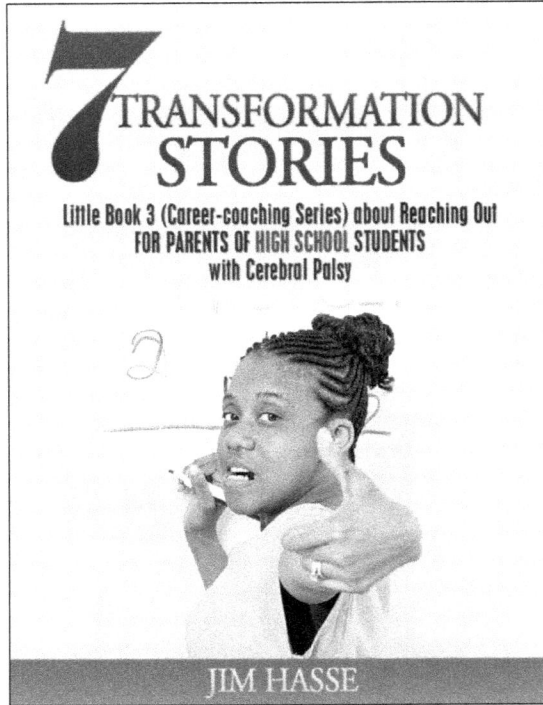

Buy **Little Book 3** on Amazon
at http://www.amazon.com/dp/B00HB77RAQ

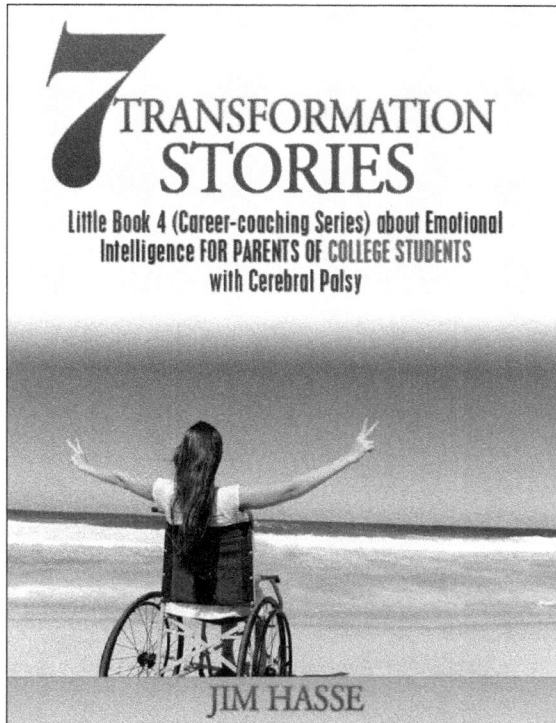

Buy **Little Book 4** on Amazon
at http://www.amazon.com/dp/B00HBDUJ96

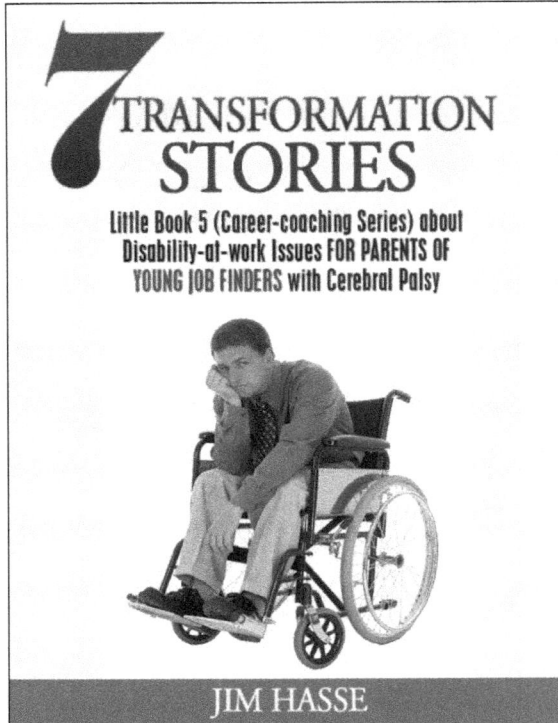

Buy **Little Book 5** on Amazon
at http://www.amazon.com/dp/B00HBVTZ02

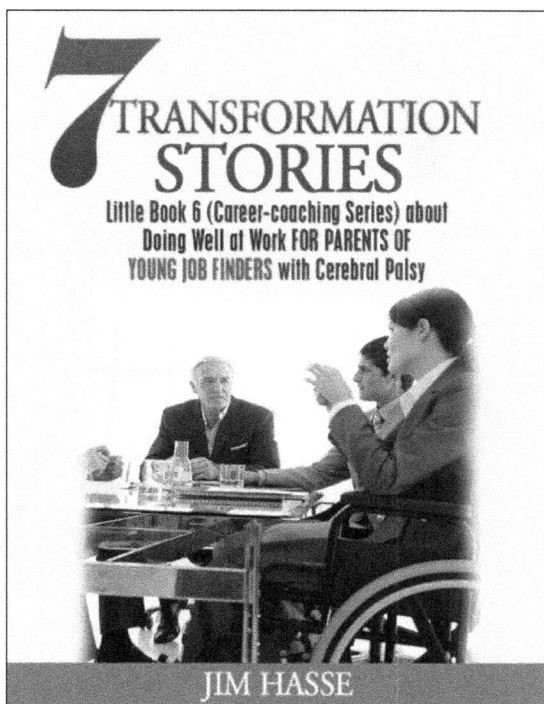

Buy **Little Book 6** on Amazon
at http://www.amazon.com/dp/B00HE60J8G

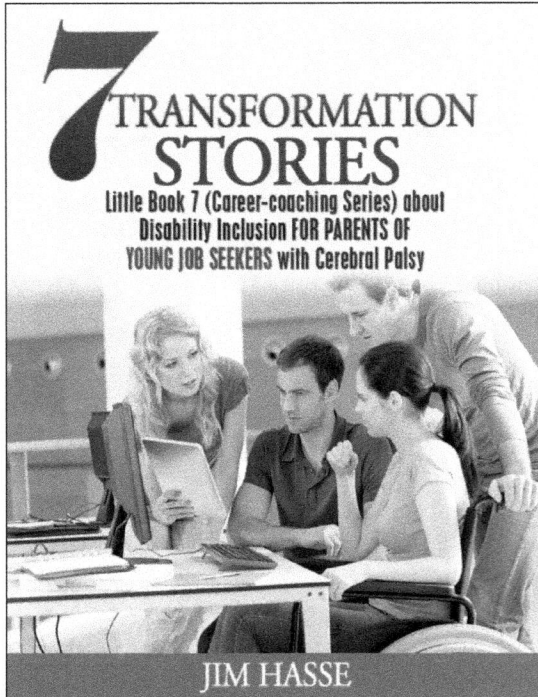

Buy **Little Book 7** on Amazon
at http://www.amazon.com/dp/B00HEVJYUU

Five Books *for* Parenting Youngsters with Special Needs

CAREER BOOK

Each of these five books (available in electronic and paperback formats) takes about 40 minutes to read. Each illustrates and summarizes the essential career development strategies to follow for your youngster's age group – all based on the roadmap recommended by National Career Development Guidelines (NCDG) and Jim Hasse's experience as a Global Career Development Facilitator and as a person with cerebral palsy and mainstream work experience.

You'll find considerably more detail about each career building strategy at www.cerebral-palsy-career-builders.com, which can be used as an ongoing reference for "how to" information as your youngster matures.

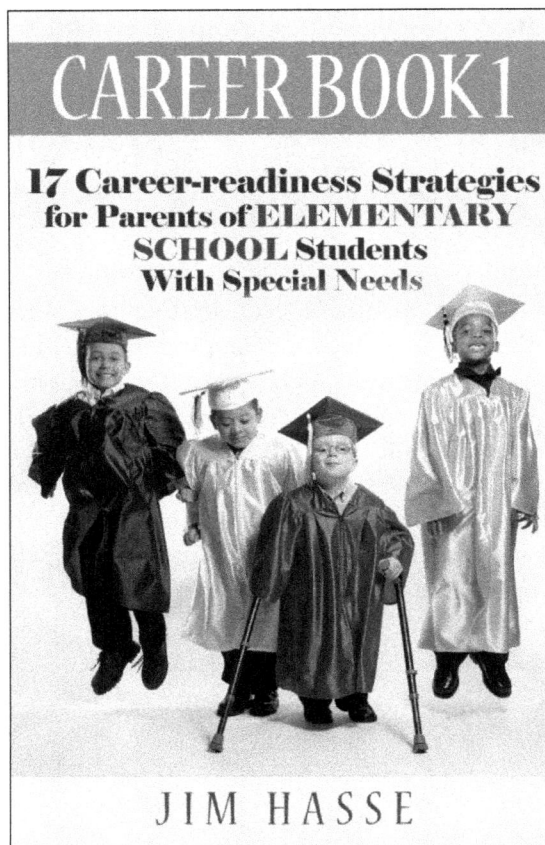

Buy **Career Book 1** on Amazon
at http://www.amazon.com/dp/B00JNYH6JM

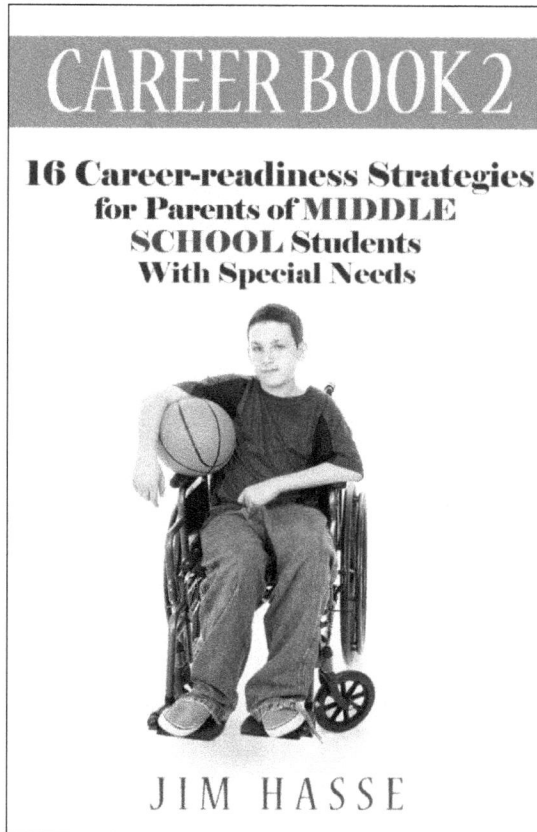

Buy **Career Book 2** on Amazon
at http://www.amazon.com/dp/B00KLIMPBS

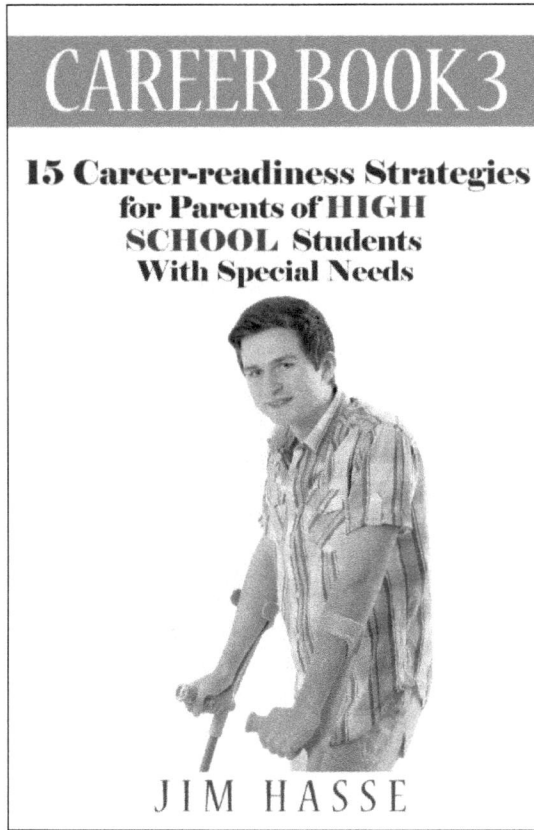

Buy **Career Book 3** on Amazon
at http://www.amazon.com/dp/B00KN2OF56

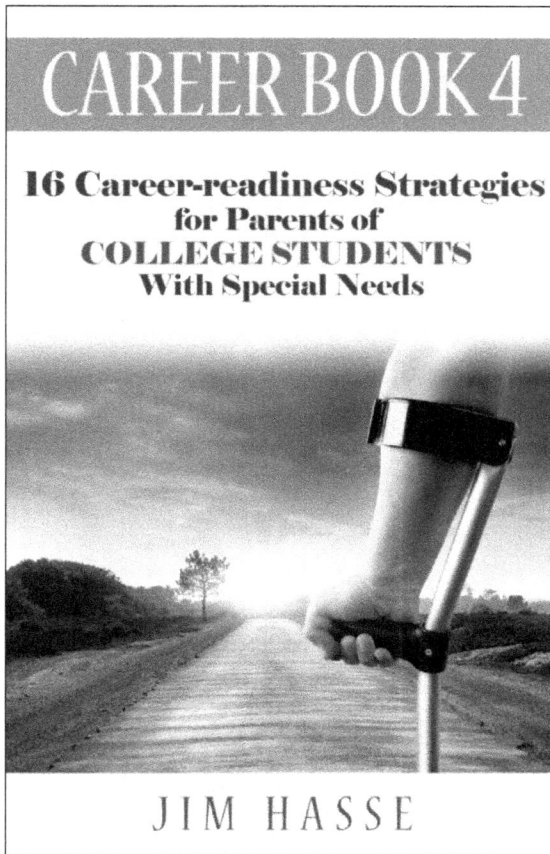

CAREER BOOK 4

16 Career-readiness Strategies for Parents of COLLEGE STUDENTS With Special Needs

JIM HASSE

Buy **Career Book 4** on Amazon
at http://www.amazon.com/dp/B00KPGV5B2

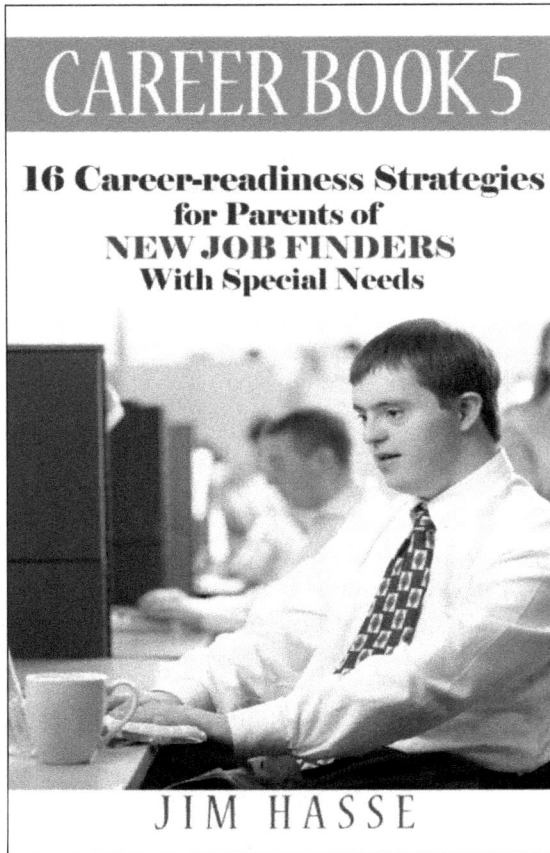

Buy **Career Book 5** on Amazon
at http://www.amazon.com/dp/B00KQRZIHC.

www.ingramcontent.com/pod-product-compliance
Lightning Source LLC
Chambersburg PA
CBHW060954040426
42445CB00011B/1154